# Hush!

## SECRETS FROM THE NATIONAL LIBRARY

# SLOBODANKA GRAHAM

# *Hush!*

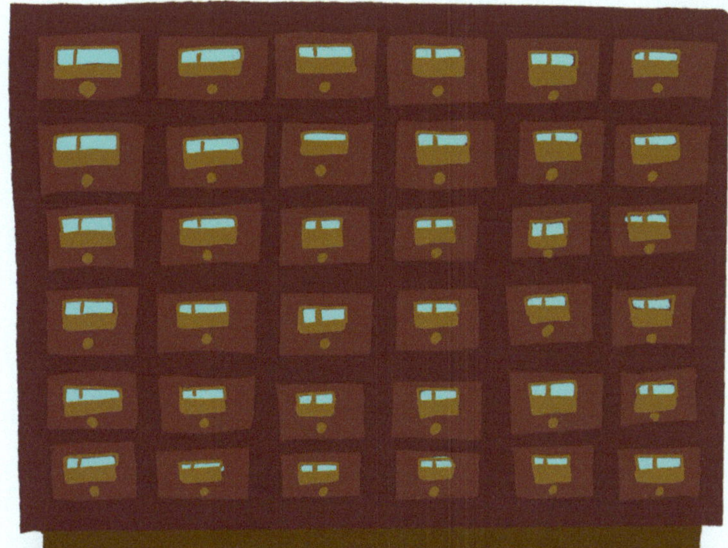

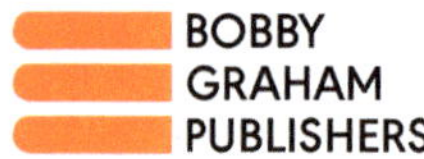


Published by BGPublishers
www.bgpublishers.com.au
© 2019 Bobby Graham Publishers
On behalf of Antipodigital
www.antipodigital.com.au



Cover and book design by Elise Knotek, Stripe Design
With illustrations by Slobodanka Graham
Author photo by Grace Costa
Digital editions produced by SunTecIndia
www.suntecindia.com

First edition 2019

ISBN 978-0-6486686-0-2 (print)
ISBN 978-0-6486686-1-9 (digital)

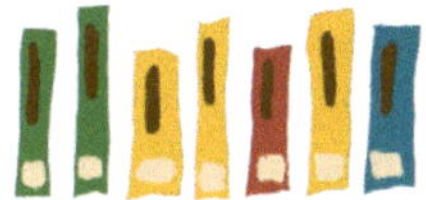

# Introduction

The National Library of Australia is a great institution and building. Step inside the foyer to experience the marbled spaciousness. Consult any of the reading rooms to enjoy expert assistance and reference materials. Sip coffee in the glow of a stained-glass window. Browse the books and select gifts in the Library shop. Wherever you turn, you are rewarded by timeless quality - not just of materials, but also of service and knowledge.

The Library staff are dedicated, impassioned, resourceful and innovative. Ask a Library staff member anything and they will respond to the best of their ability - and offer more assistance.

I worked at the National Library from 2005 to 2010, initially as Web Content Manager then as Director Web Publishing. This was a time of innovation and digital development. We combined technology and Library resources in new and exciting ways. The Library continues, decade after decade, to produce innovative services. It does this while maintaining and providing access for all Australians to our literary and pictorial history and culture.

Late in 2018, I was contracted by the Library to assist with a website refresh. During this time, I re-engaged with staff, former colleagues, and the building. From March to June 2019, I took advantage of my time at the Library to visit little-known corners of the building, sketching people and places that caught my eye. During my lunch hour, I sat surreptitiously in corridors, iPad on my knee, trying not to look and feel silly as I quickly sketched what I saw. Eventually staff became used to me and we chatted over my most recent sketch.

This little book of illustrations is not a definitive guide to the Library. It is simply my idiosyncratic attempt to showcase spaces - some, like the book stacks, only accessible to staff members. But I've also tried to capture the qualities of the readings rooms, and all those people who use them.

I thank the National Library for providing me with this opportunity: the ideal venue for my homage to the building and all those who work in it. And of course the reading room patrons who were my unwitting subjects - I thank you as well.

SLOBODANKA
GRAHAM
September 2019

# Welcome to the National Library of Australia

*A place for all Australians to enjoy our heritage and culture.*

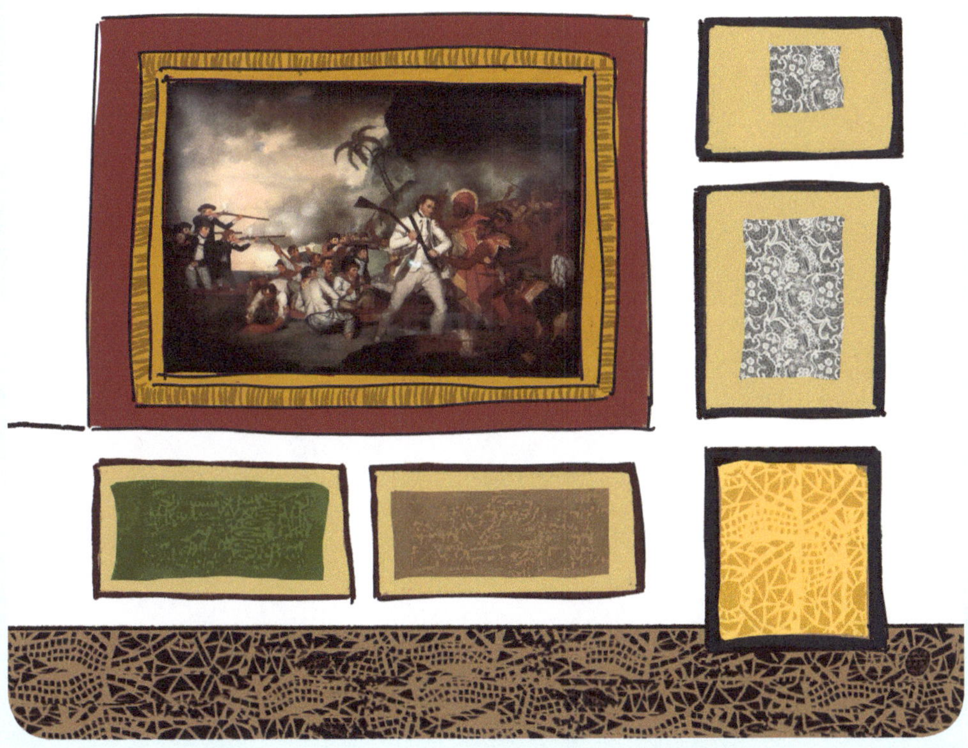

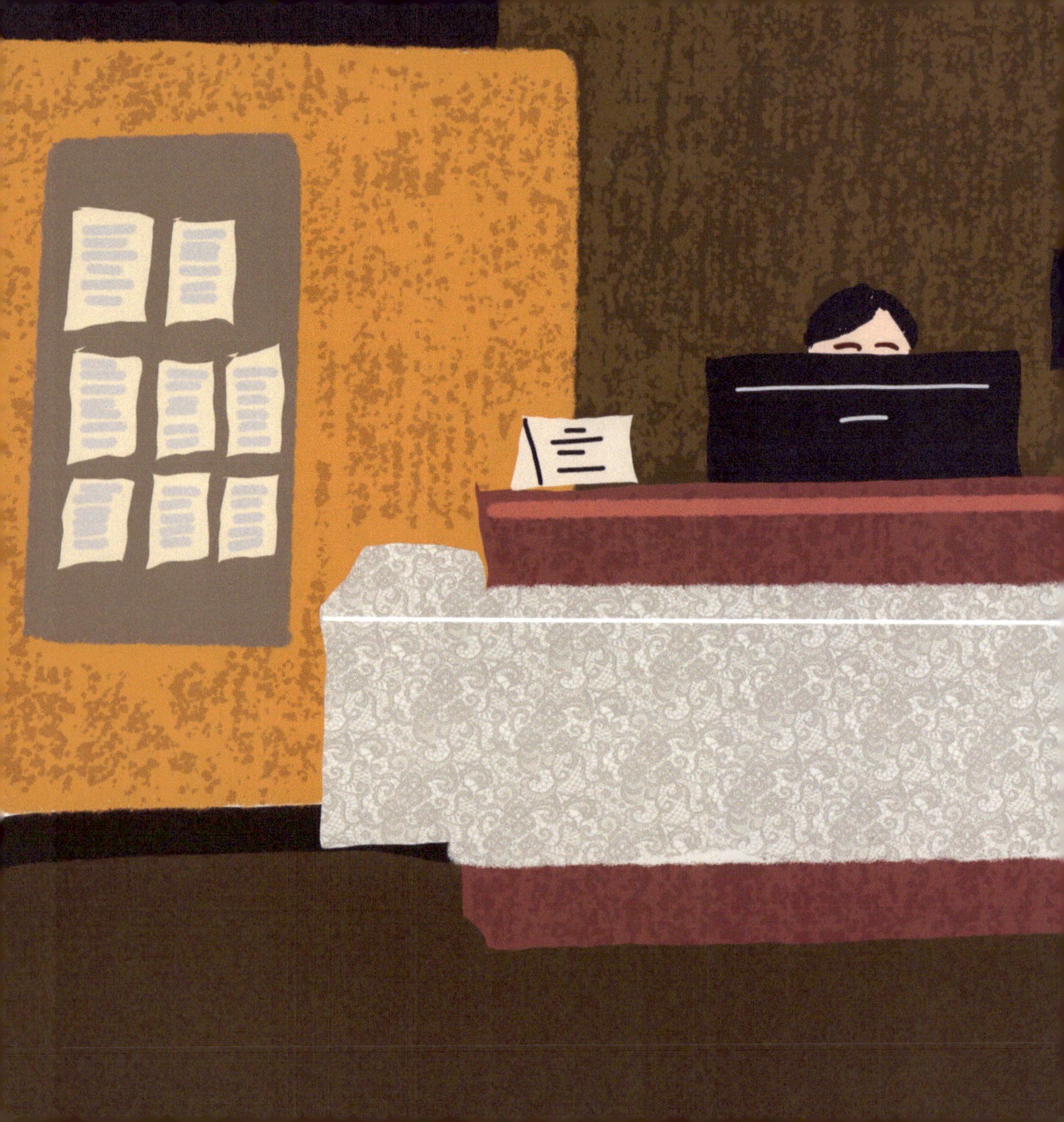

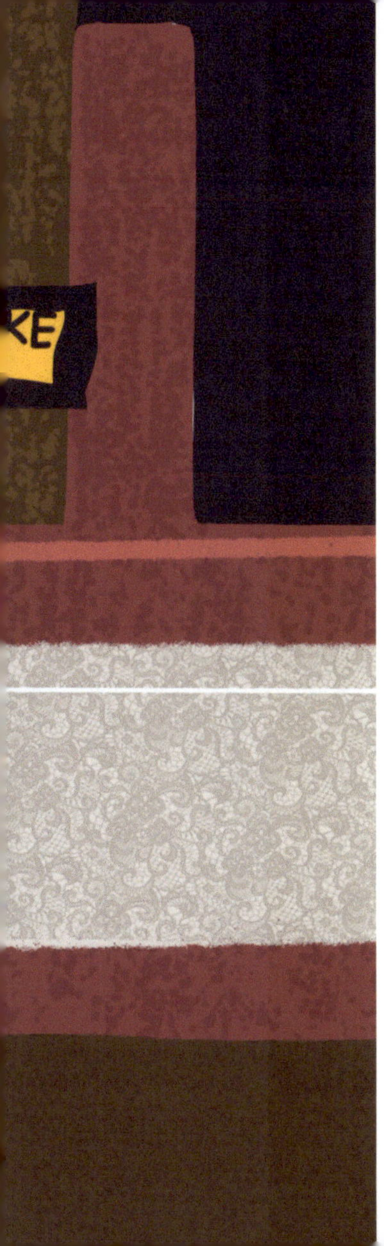

KE




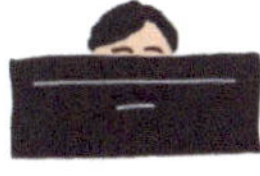

Did you know?

The Main Reading
Room is a large
and inspiring
space. It has
comfortable
seating, desks
and computers.
You can sit, read,
research online -
or simply reflect.

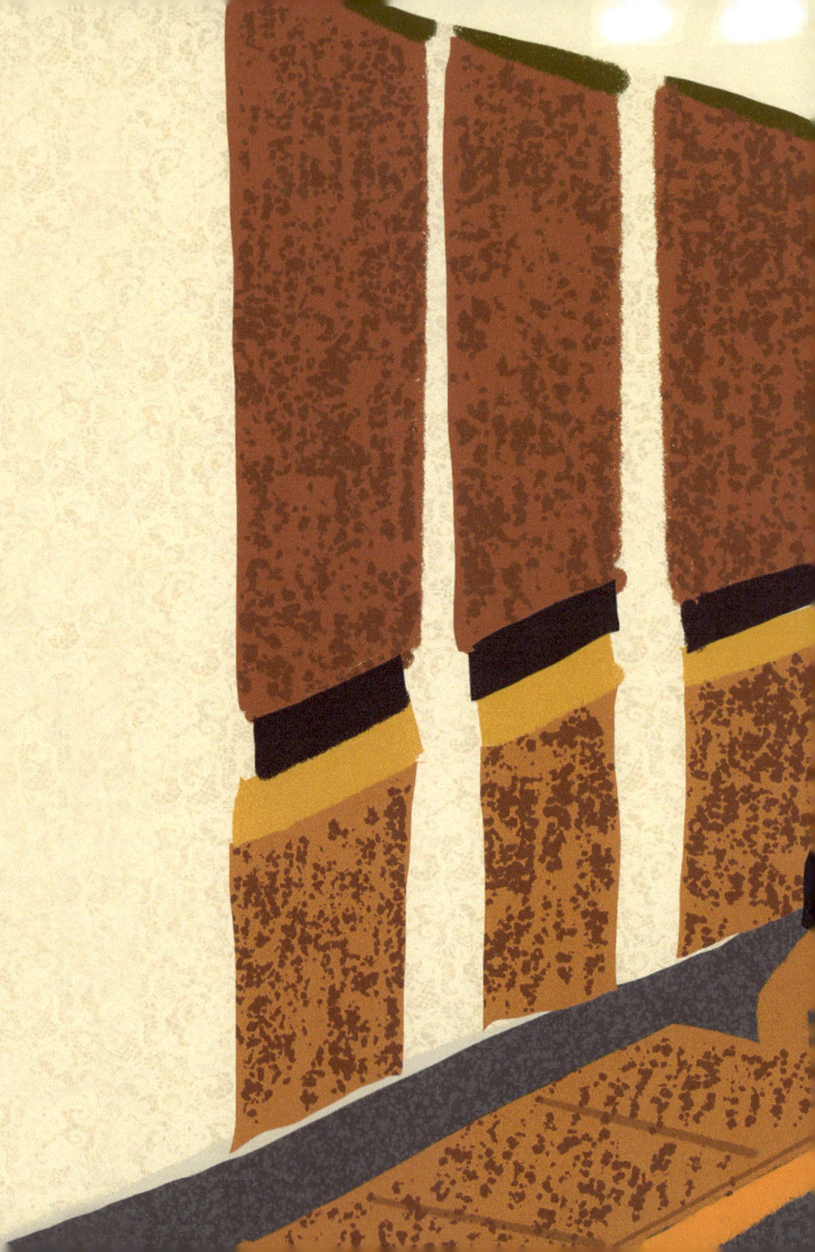

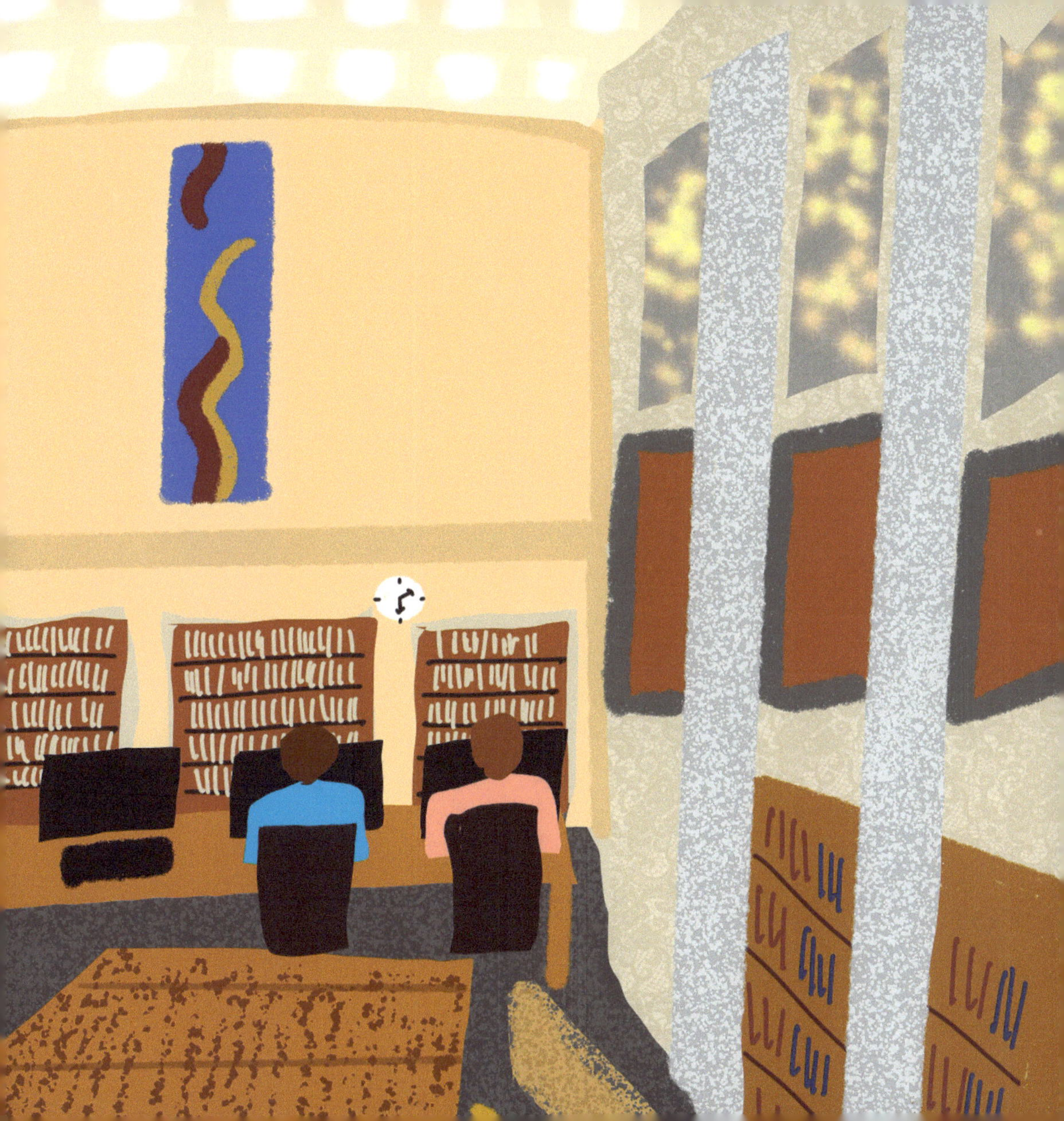

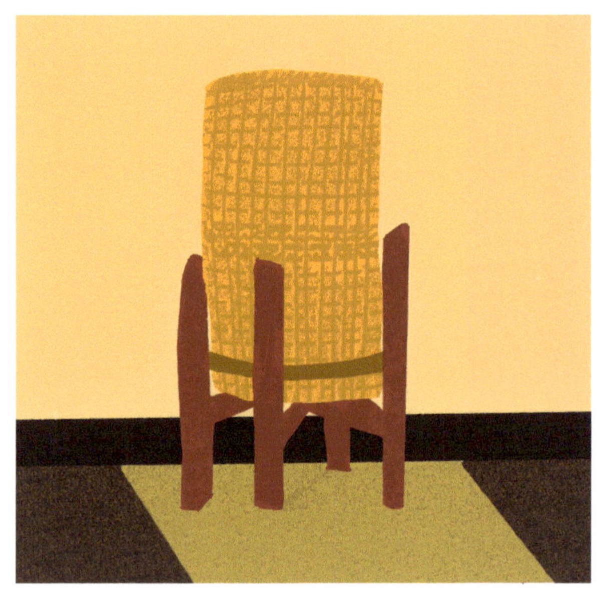

**Did you know?**

*In 1968, Fred Ward designed cane
wastepaper baskets, which are still
in use throughout the Library.*

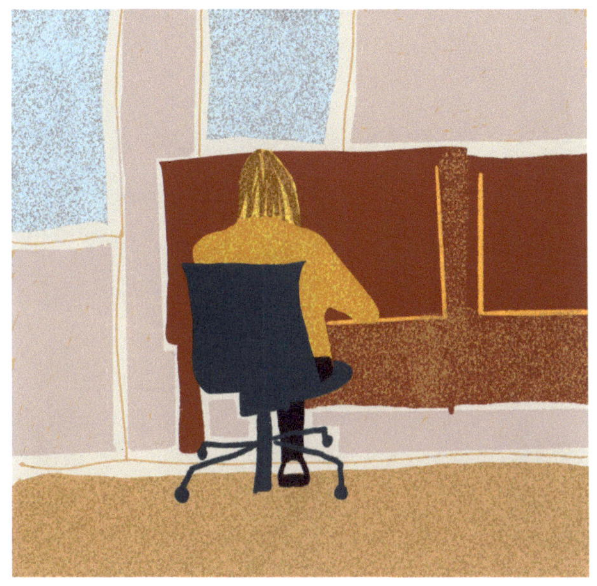

**Did you know?**

*All Library services are freely available to everyone. You can sit, read and research in the Main Reading Room.*

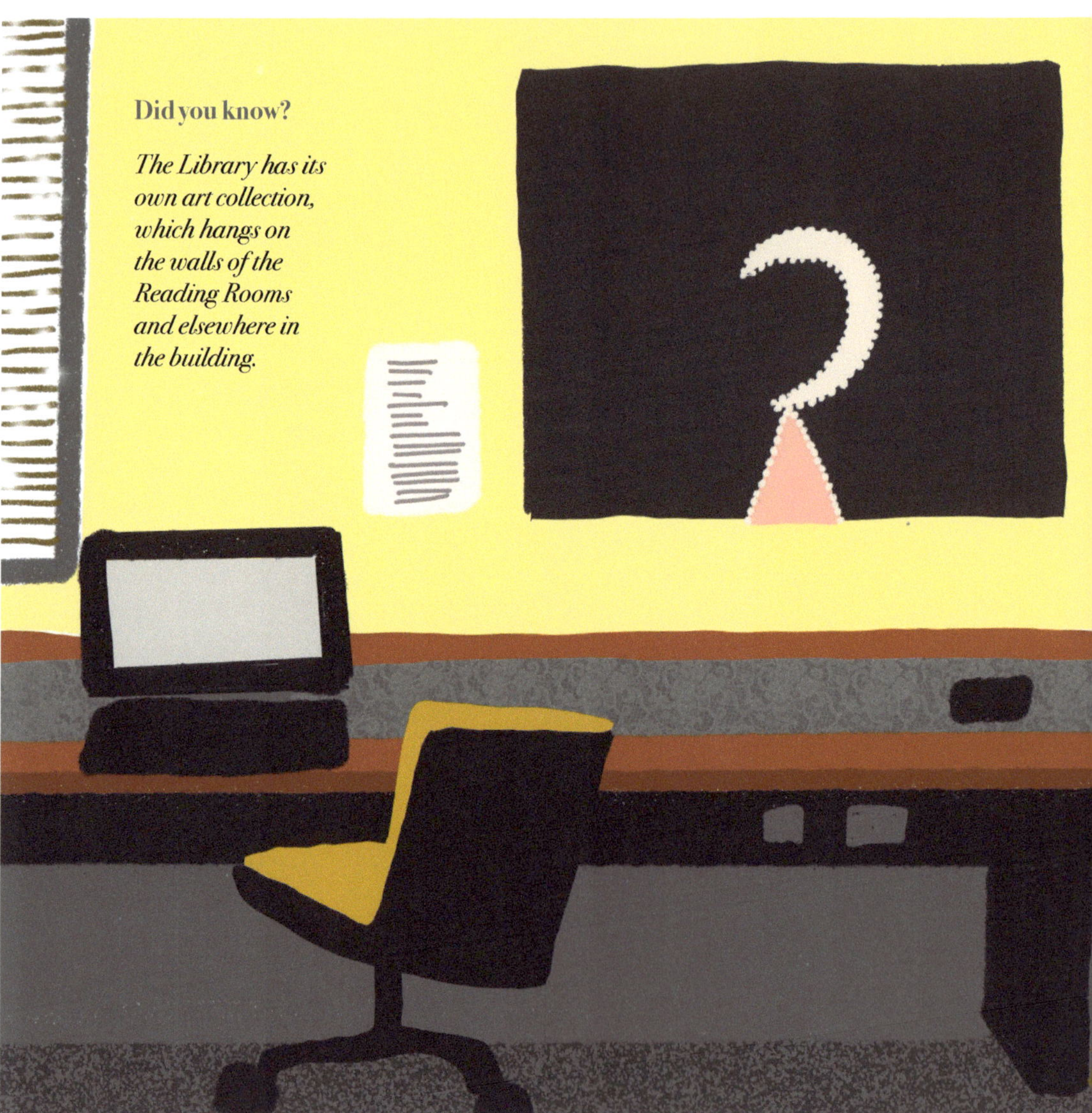

**Did you know?**

*The Library has its own art collection, which hangs on the walls of the Reading Rooms and elsewhere in the building.*

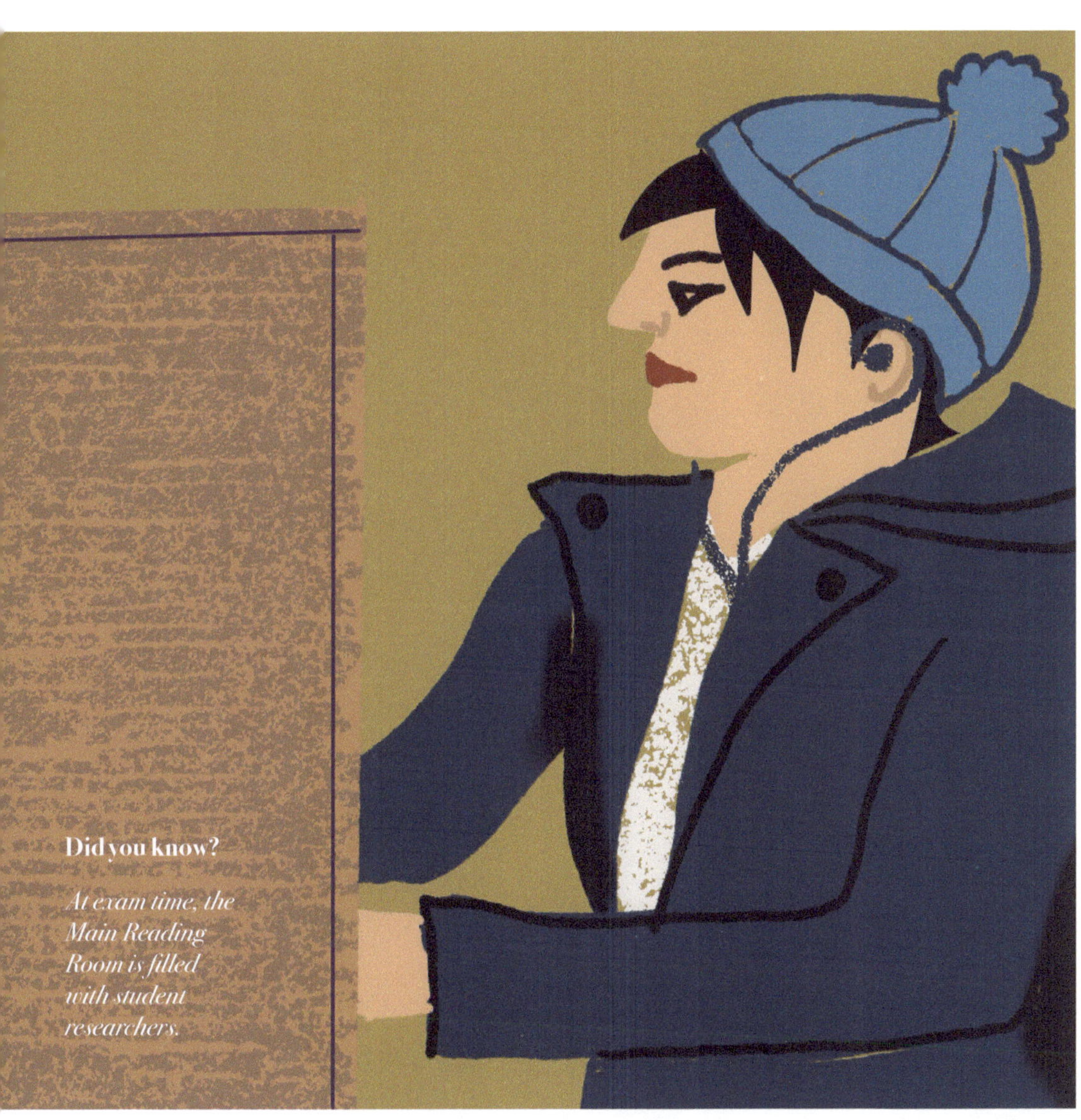

Did you know?

At exam time, the
Main Reading
Room is filled
with student
researchers.

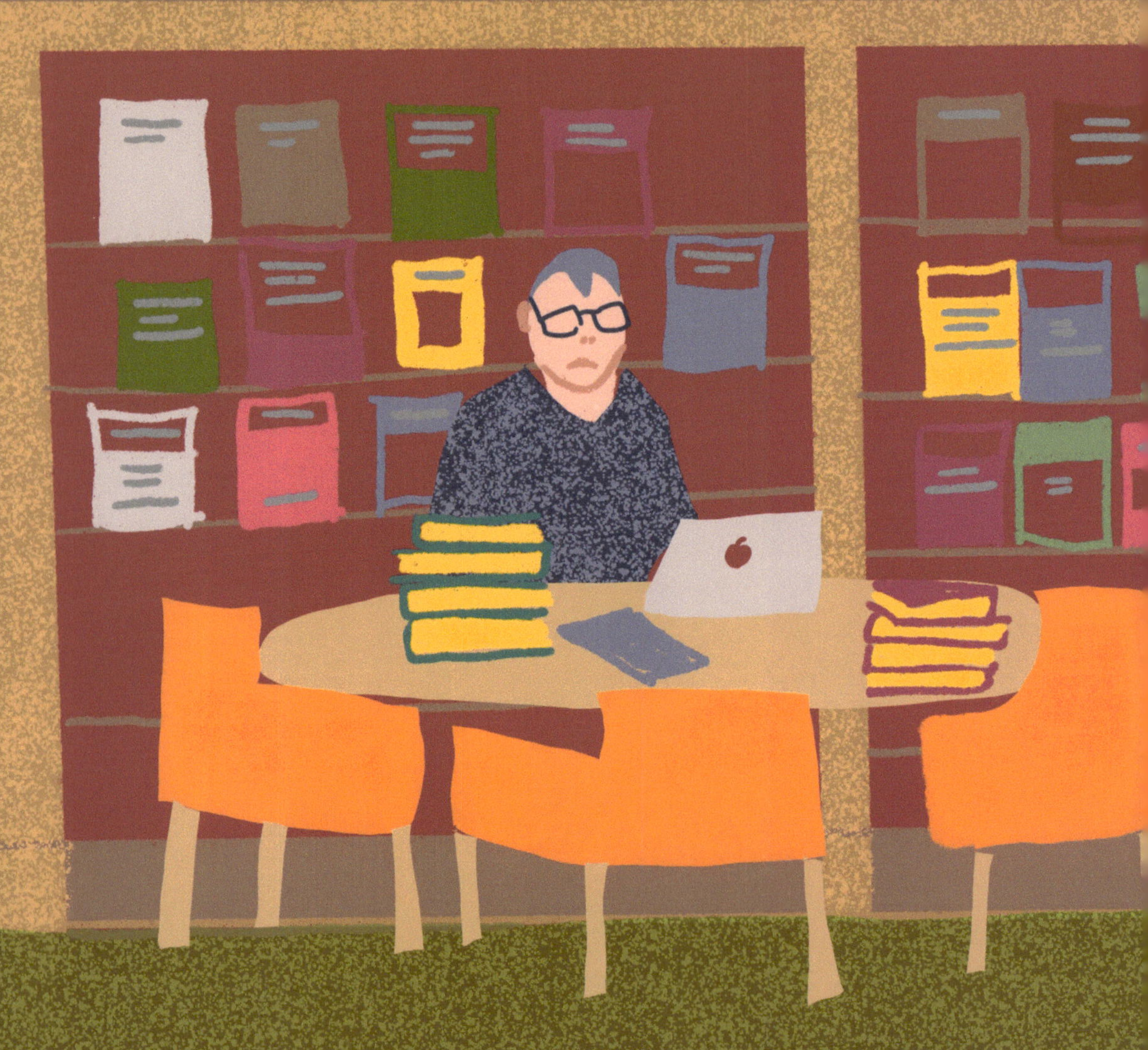

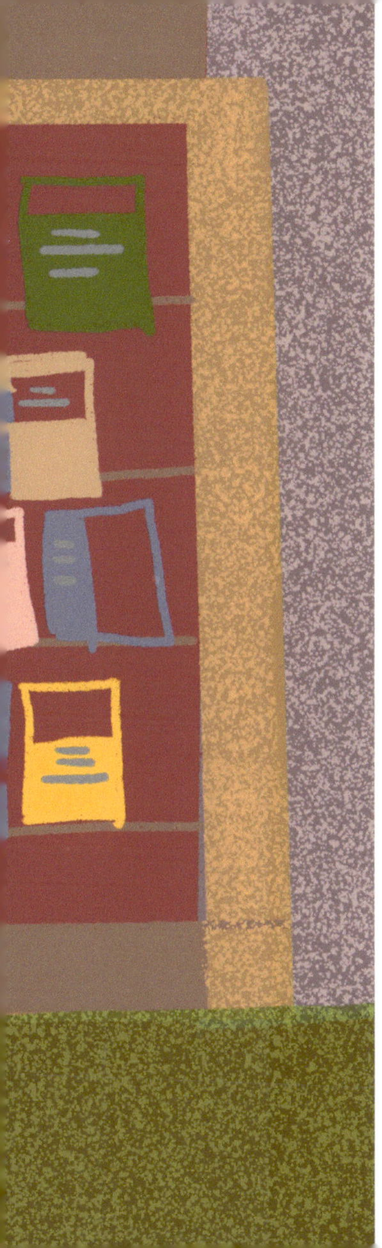



## Did you know?

*The Library collects and makes available all sorts of content - not just books. This man is reading and researching in front of the serials and magazine racks in the Main Reading Room.*

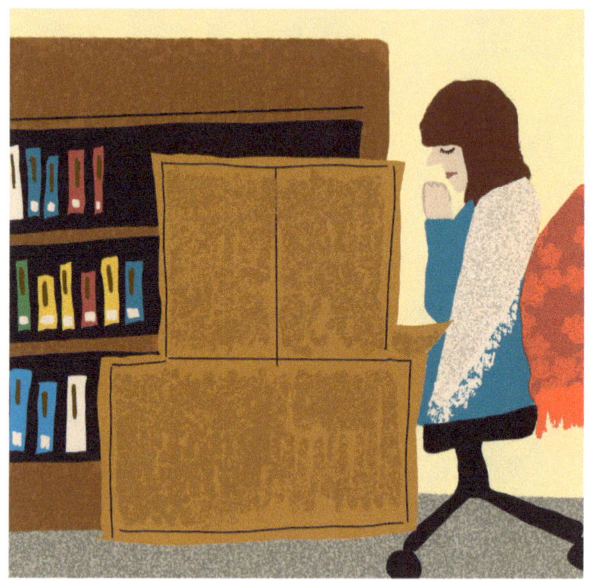

### Did you know?

*Each year the Library has over 550,000 visitors to the building. And more than 3.6 million visitors online. Almost 120,000 individual items are delivered to Library users in the Reading Rooms, or through inter-library loans.*

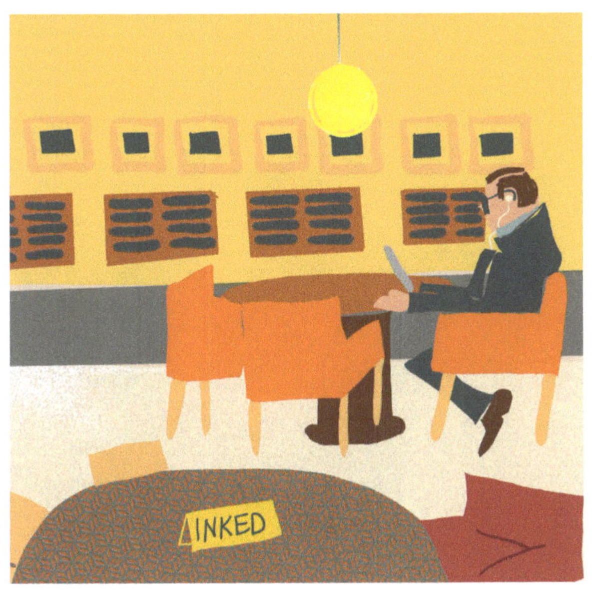

### Did you know?

*The Library has a vast collection of resources for all family historians. You can search digitised newspapers, journals, photographs and books to find out more about your own family.*

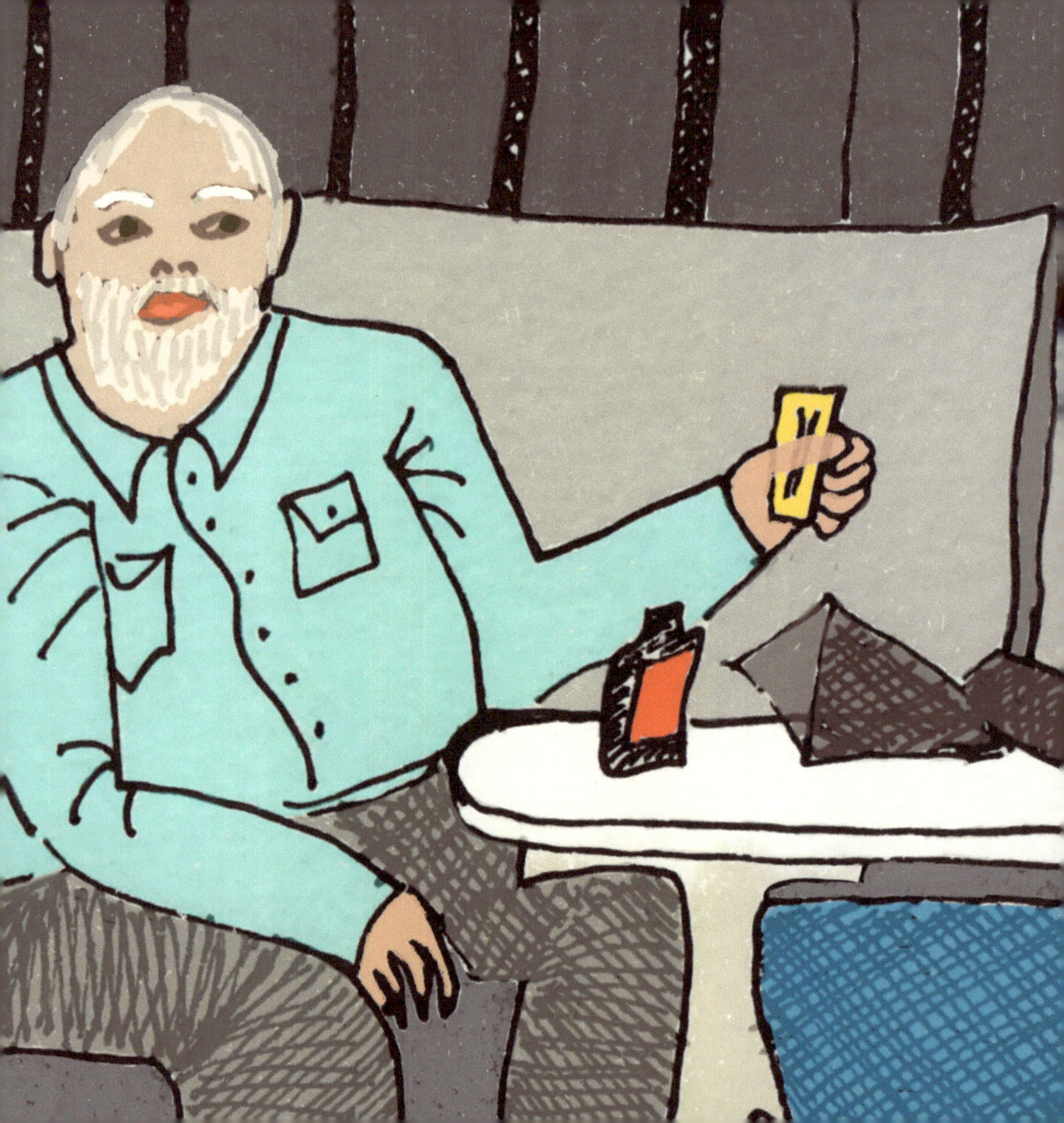

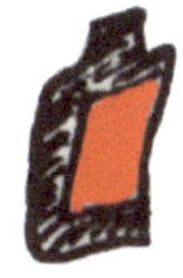

### Did you know?

*If you would like a coffee or lunch, the Library has a restaurant and a cafe.*

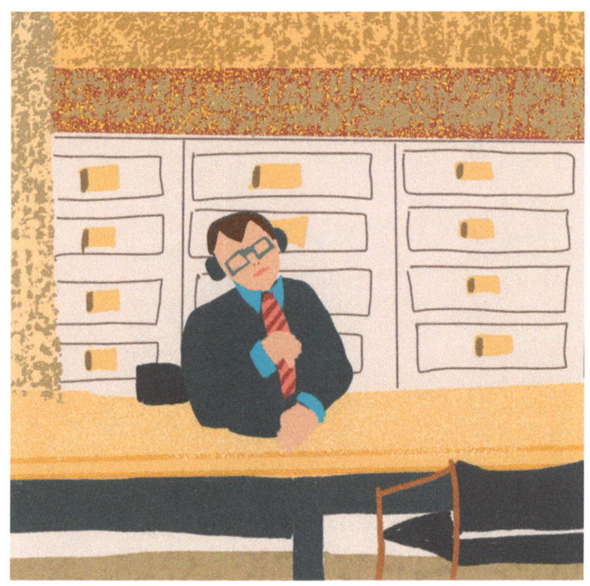

**Did you know?**

*The Library has 45,000 hours of audio recordings. You can listen to interviews, songs, even environmental sounds. Enjoy these in the Library. And many of the recordings are online.*

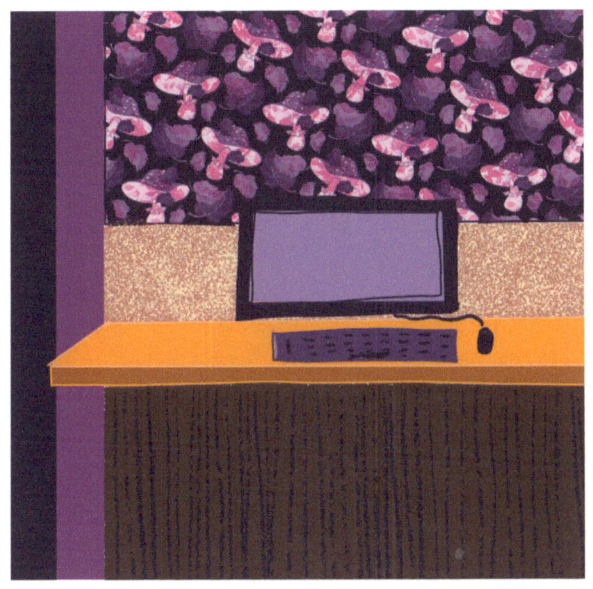


Did you know?

The Library was recently
refurbished. One of the new features
is this fabric wall covering in the
Main Reading Room.

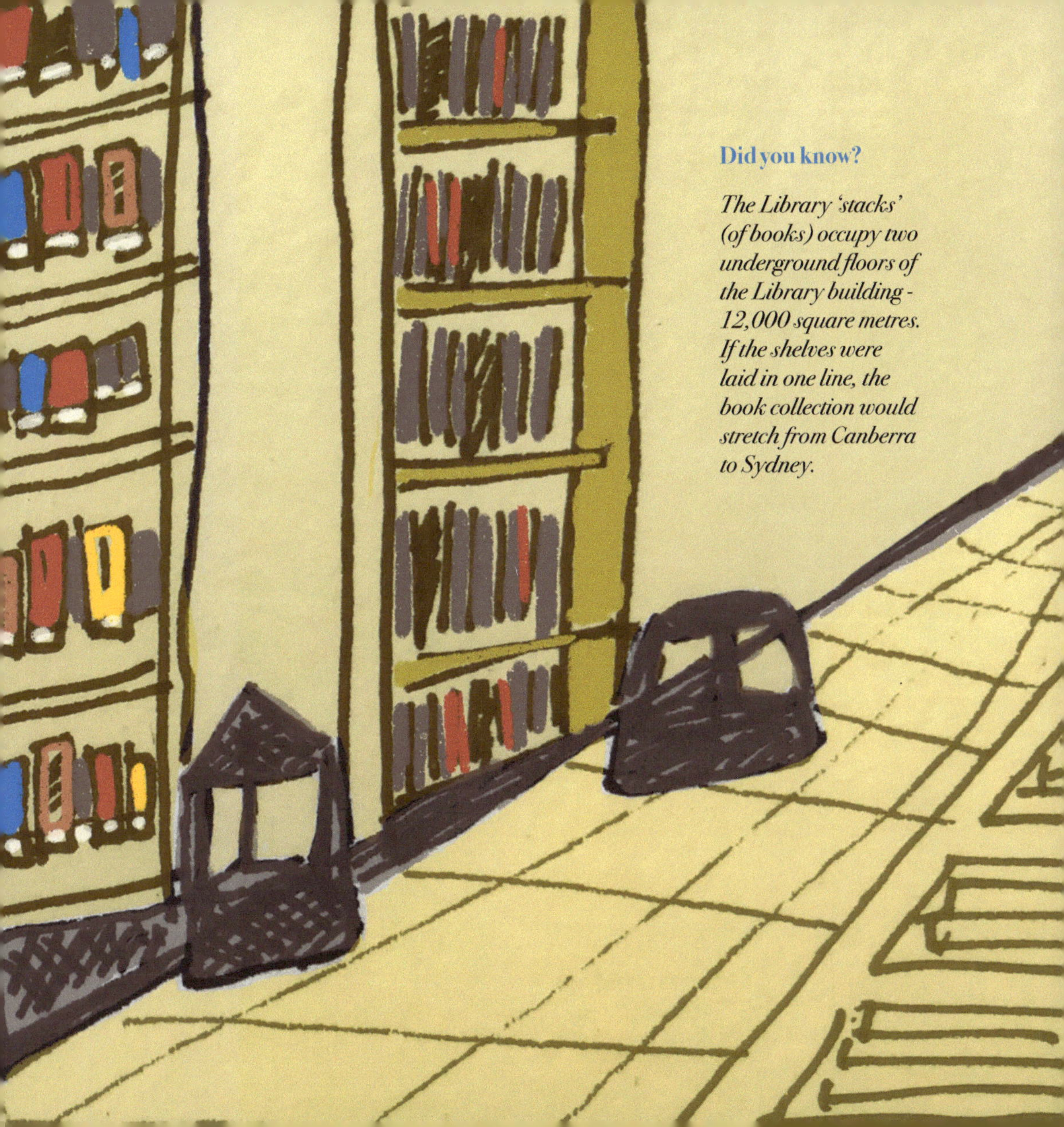


Did you know?

The Library 'stacks'
(of books) occupy two
underground floors of
the Library building -
12,000 square metres.
If the shelves were
laid in one line, the
book collection would
stretch from Canberra
to Sydney.

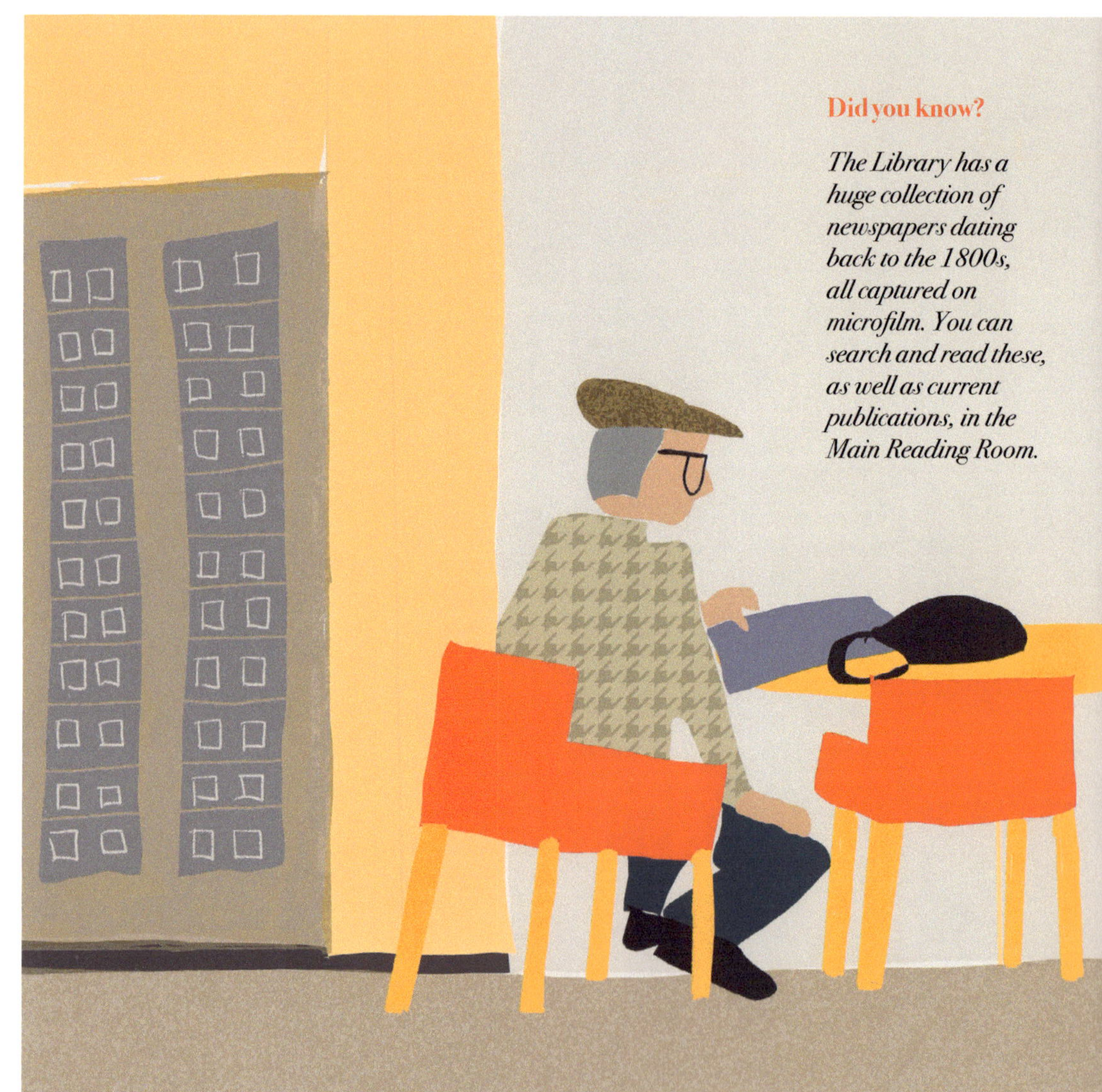


Did you know?

The Library has a
huge collection of
newspapers dating
back to the 1800s,
all captured on
microfilm. You can
search and read these,
as well as current
publications, in the
Main Reading Room.

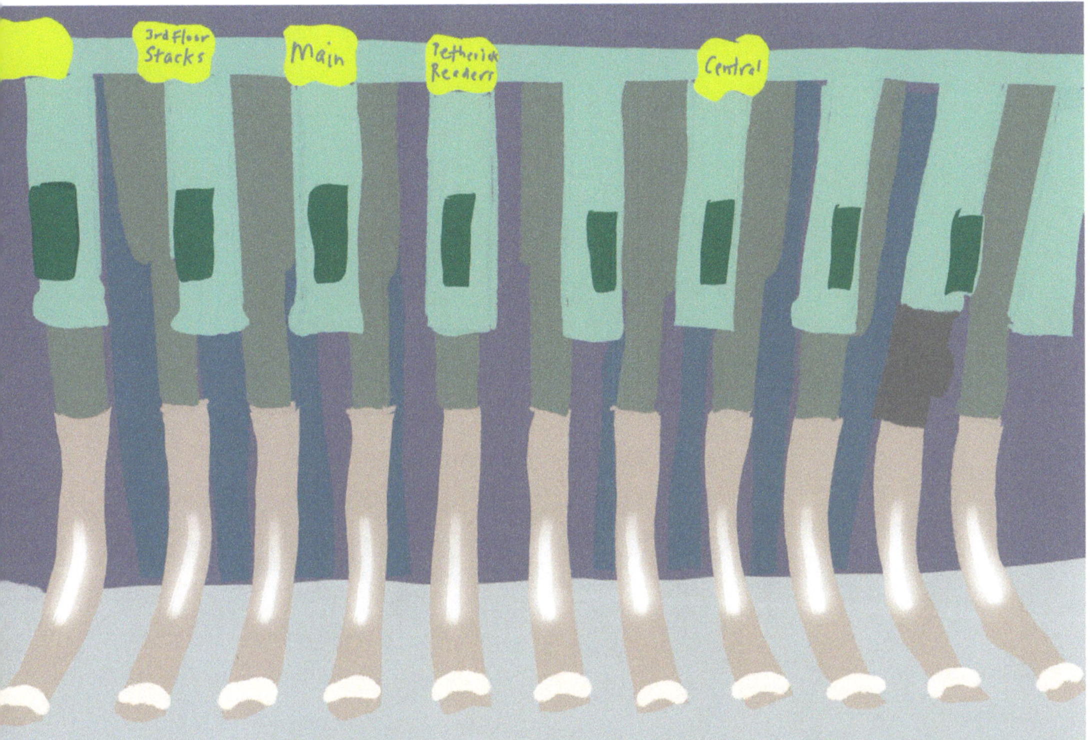


### Did you know?

*In the old days, book requests in the Main Reading Room were sent to the book stacks through chutes. The chutes are still in working order, but are no longer used other than to show schoolchildren how they work. Book requests are now all performed online.*

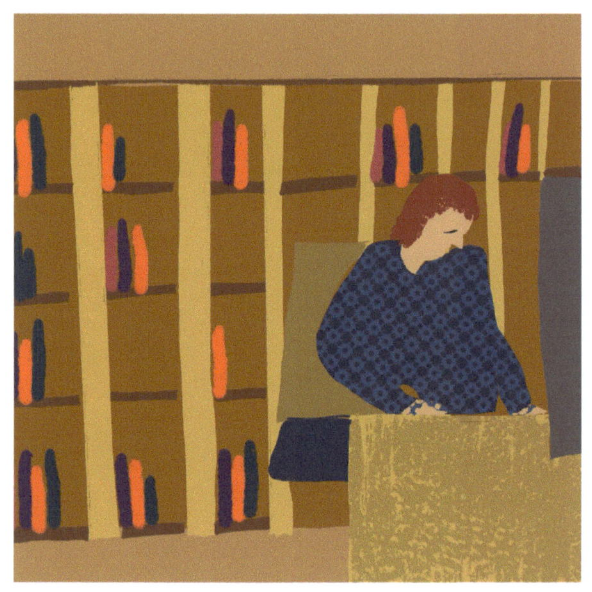

### Did you know?

*As a Petherick Room Reader, you
get privileged access to the Library
collections. This means you can
study original documents yourself.*

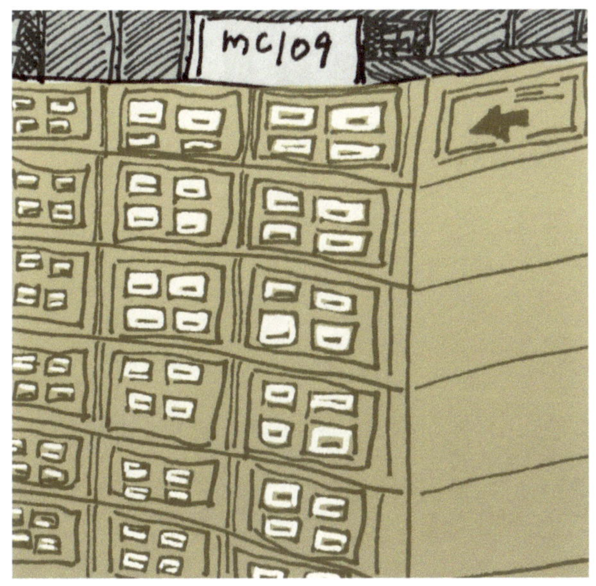


### Did you know?

*Newspapers take up a lot of space - and are very fragile. Which is why the Library has preserved newspapers in microfilm. The microfilm reels are safely stored in underground cabinets.*

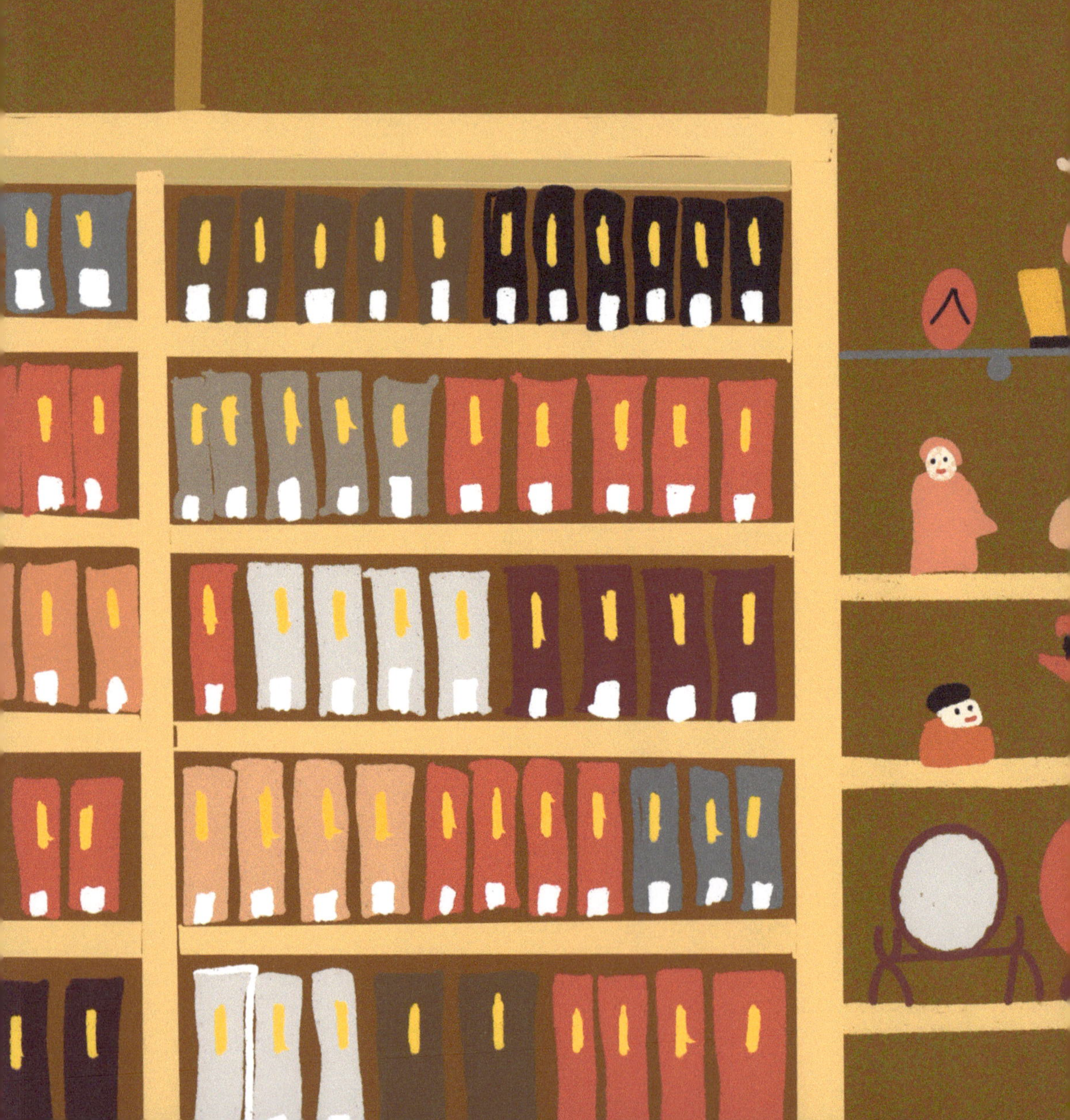

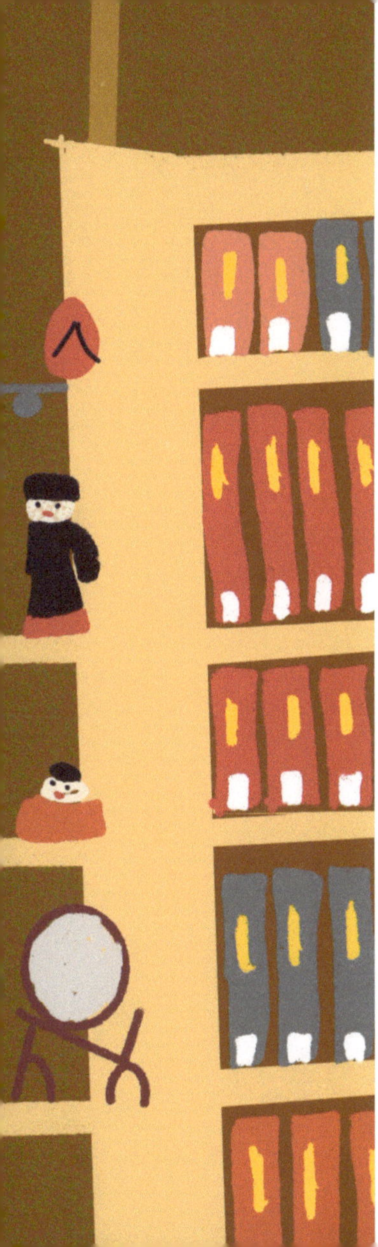



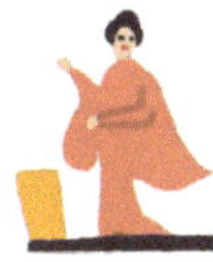

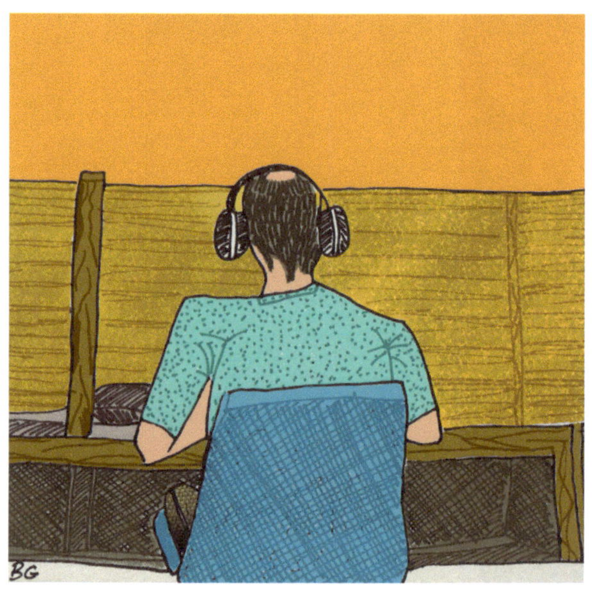



## Did you know?

*Use your Library card to request a book.*
*You can read or study in the Main Reading Room.*

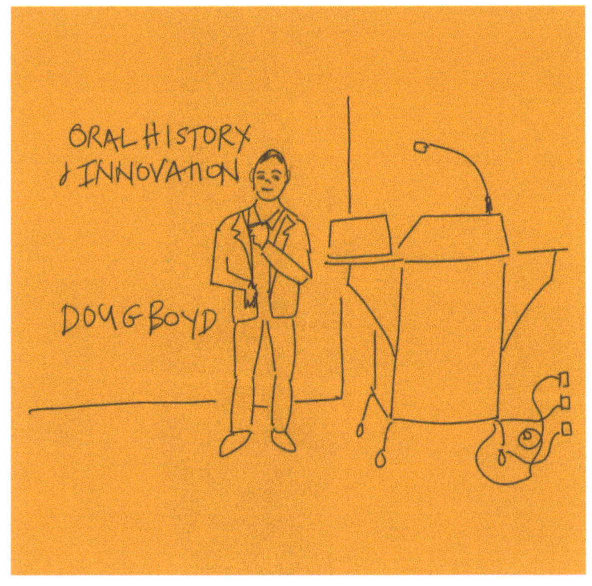


**Did you know?**

*You can attend many lectures, book talks
and presentations at the Library.*

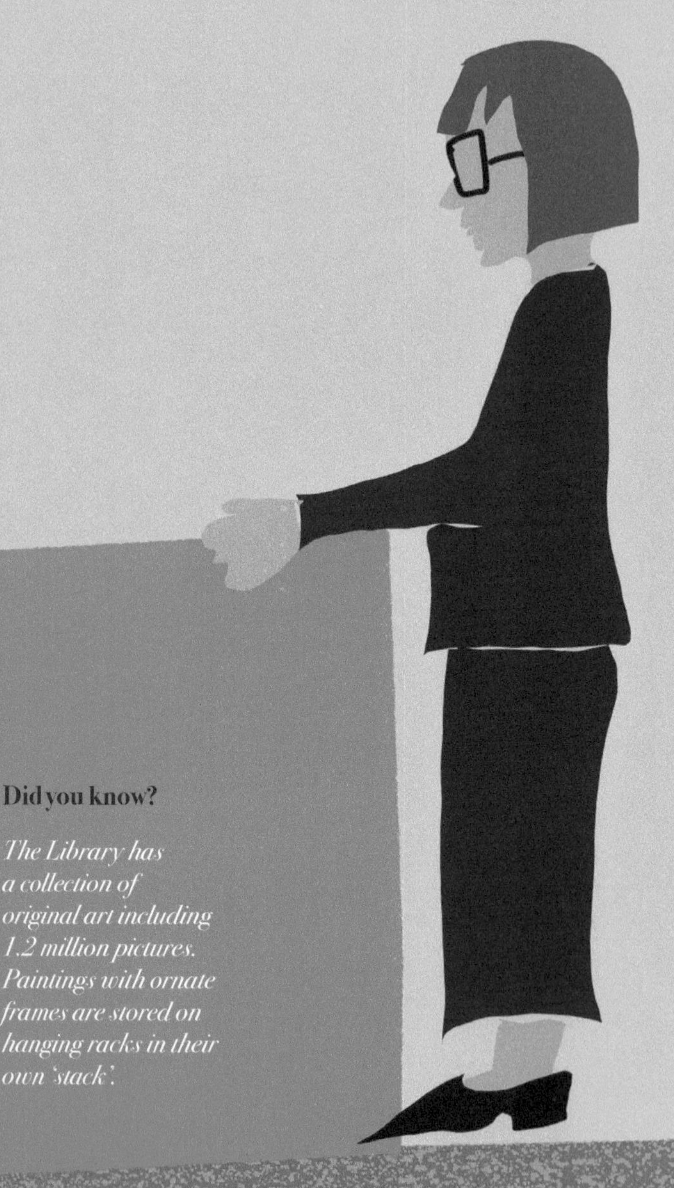


Did you know?

The Library has
a collection of
original art including
1.2 million pictures.
Paintings with ornate
frames are stored on
hanging racks in their
own 'stack'.

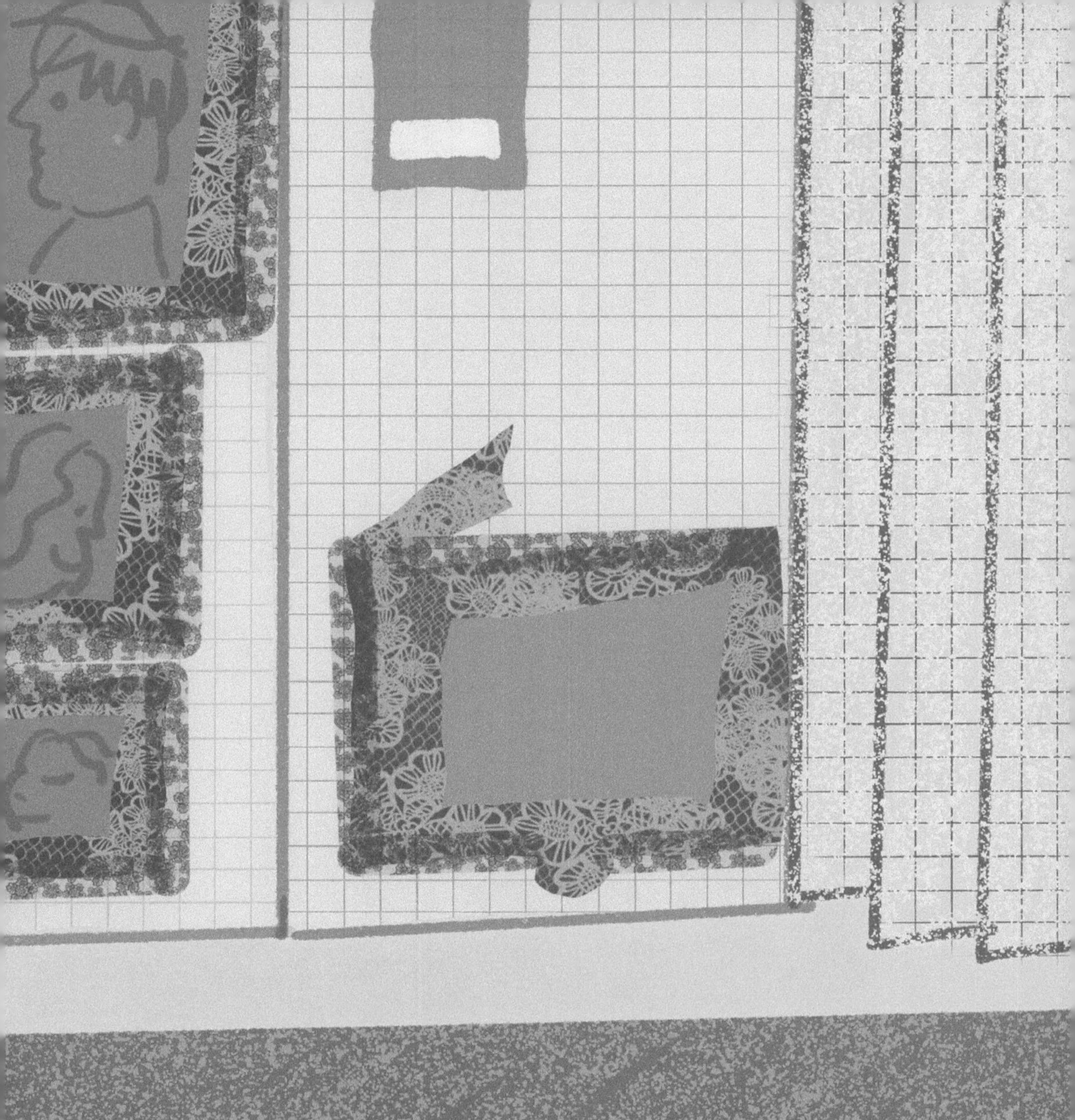

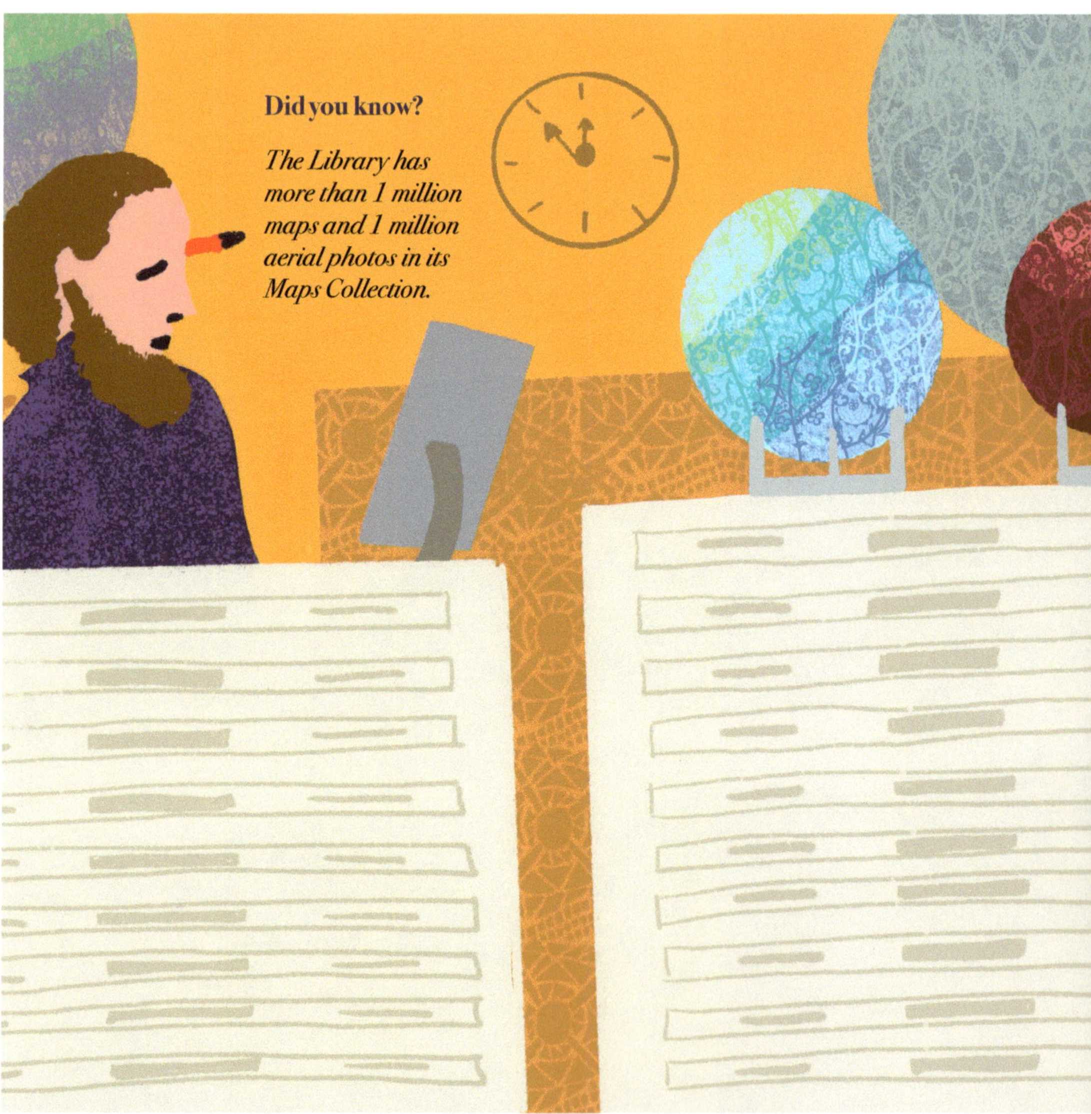
Did you know?

The Library has more than 1 million maps and 1 million aerial photos in its Maps Collection.

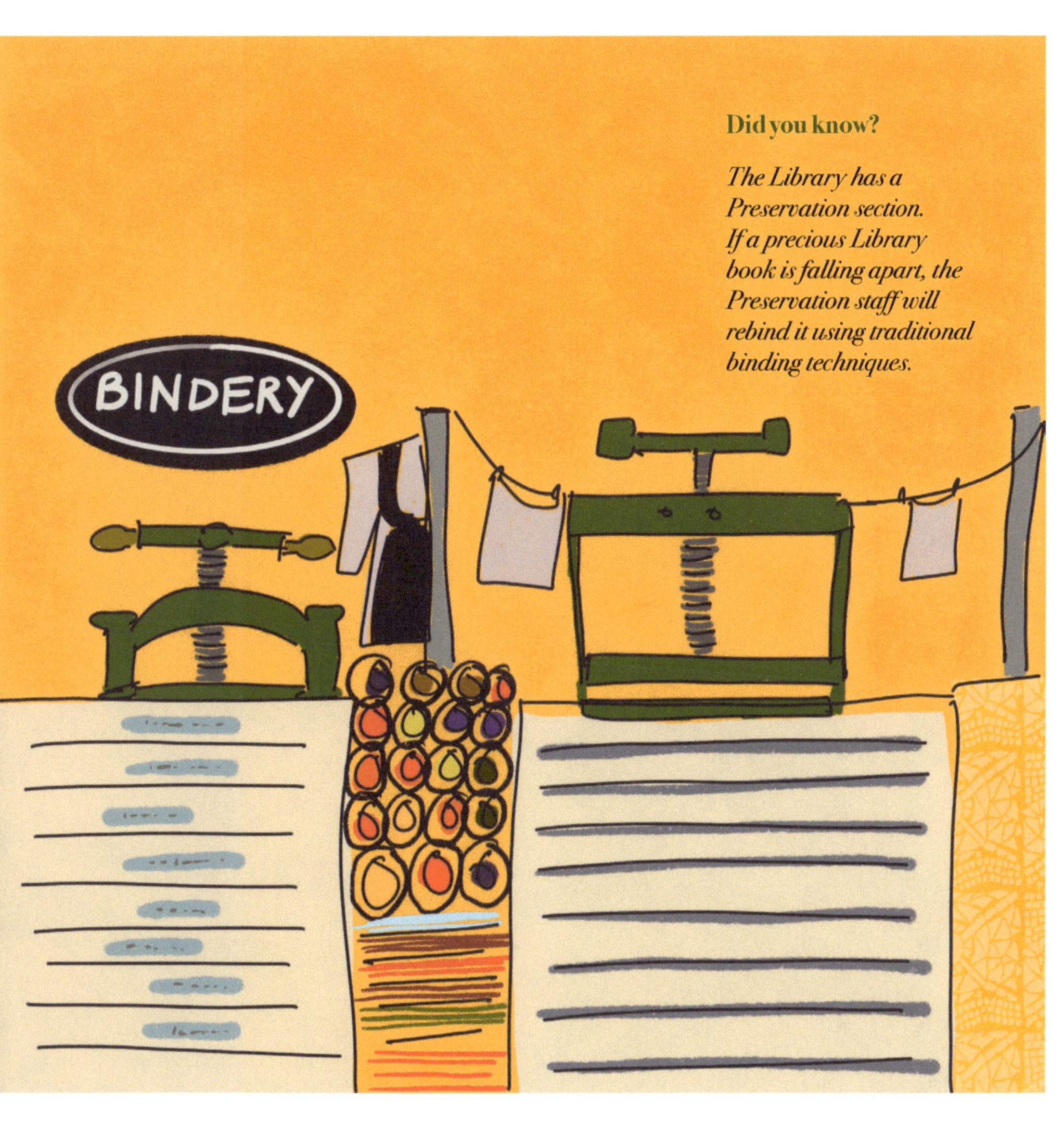
BINDERY

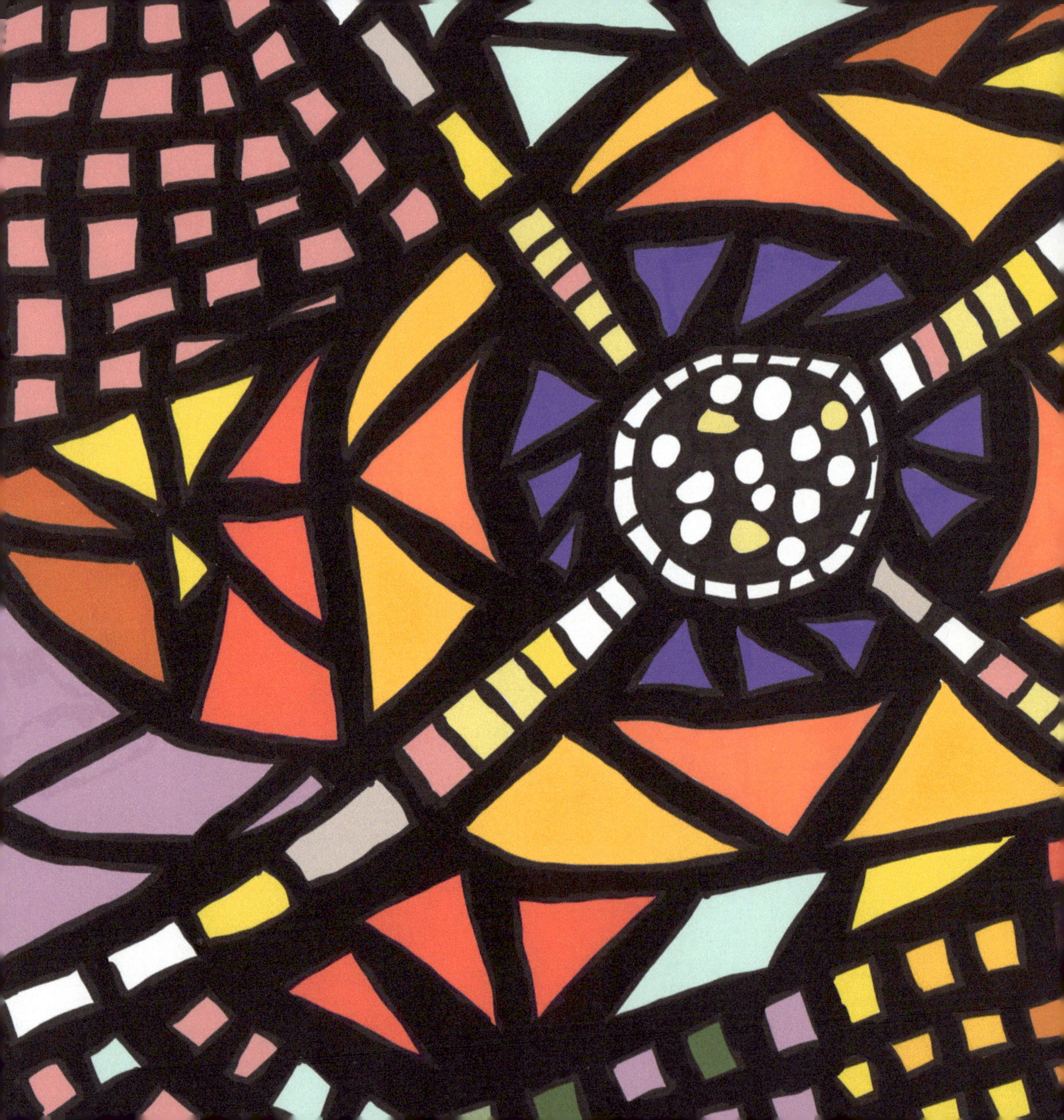

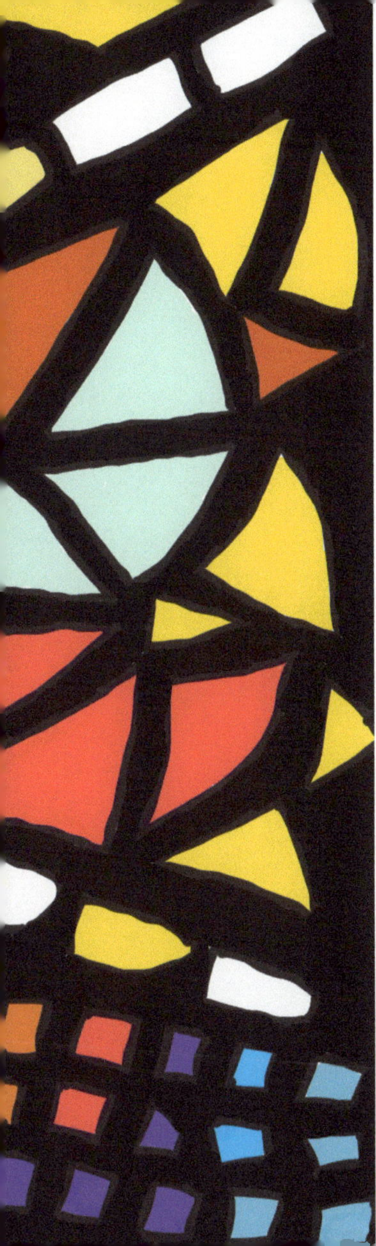



**Did you know?**

*There are 16 stained glass windows by Leonard French. The Belgian and French glass blocks refract and maximise the light. Enjoy more than 50 colours that flood the Library foyer.*

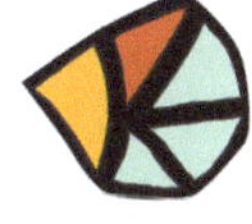

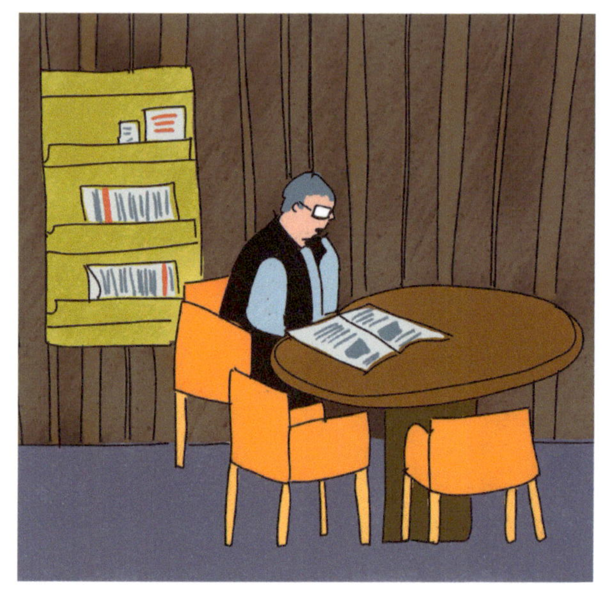

### Did you know?

*The Library Reading Rooms are used by staff as well as the public. Each day Paul takes time out of his busy schedule to page through a newspaper during his lunch hour.*

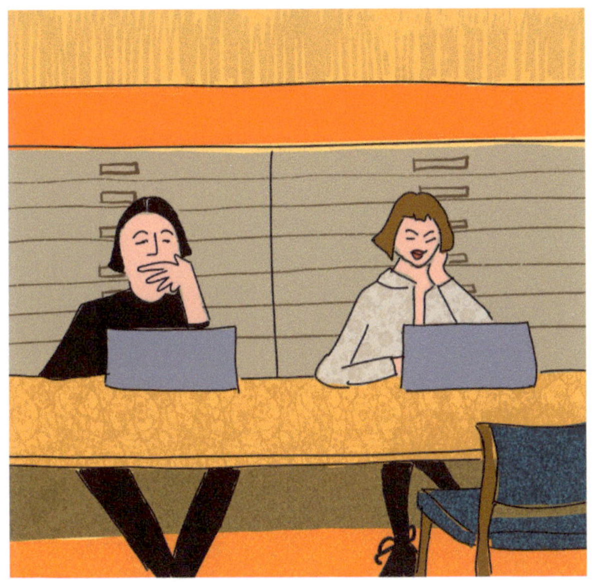

**Did you know?**

*All sorts of people use the Library Reading Rooms: family historians, academics, hobbyists, older people and younger people like this couple. They were absorbed in their work but seemed to enjoy spending time together as well.*

**Did you know?**

*The Library supports learning, creative and intellectual endeavour, and contributes to the continuing vitality of Australia's diverse culture and heritage. But it does more than that. It provides all Australians a space to appreciate and enjoy its many valued services.*

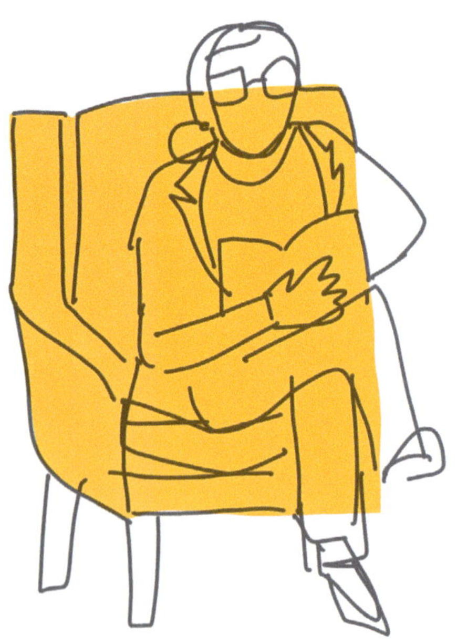

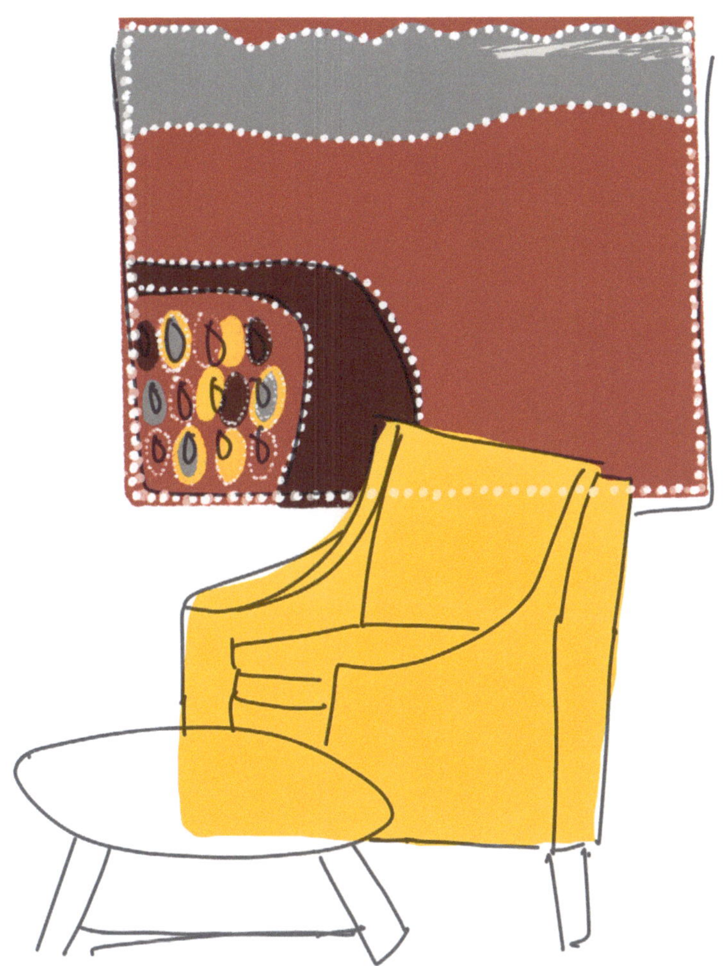

# More from this author

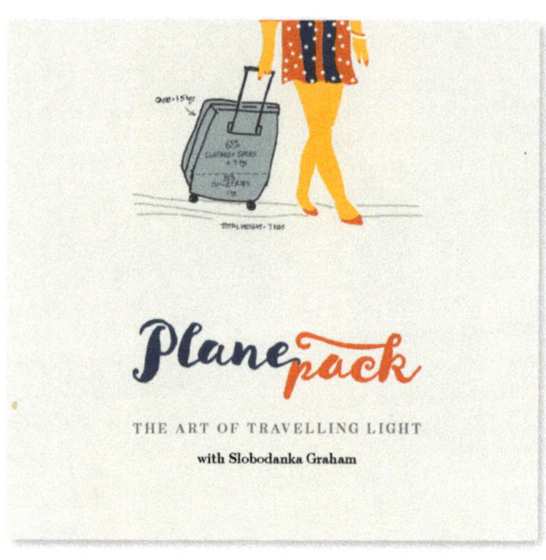


**I fly and travel with carry-on luggage only. That's 7kgs. And yes, you can do it too!**

At Planepack, discover the art of light travel: skip the queues; hop in and out of trains, boats and planes. Lose your addiction to heavy cases and you too will be a liberated light traveller.

I write, review, and illustrate light travel essentials, packing guides, travel tips - and how to travel with style and ease.

I hope *Planepack: the art of travelling light* inspires *you* to travel light.

**www.planepack.com.au**